DANDELION
CLOCKS POEMS
BY NICHOLAS CAMPBELL

PHOENIX PRESS

DANDELION
CLOCKS POEMS
BY NICHOLAS CAMPBELL

Acknowledgments

Some of these poems have previously appeared in the following magazines and periodicals to whose editors grateful acknowledgment is made: *Bakunin, Asylum, Tsunami, Café Solo, Poetry LA, the Los Angeles Times Book Review, Poetry Salzburg Review, Corners of the Mouth Anthology, The Rogue Voice, The Sunflower Collective, Garden Street Press, Blue Monday Review* and *America, the National Catholic Review,* published by *America Media.*

Cover design by Nicholas Campbell. All photographs are Public Domain images or from Campbell and Yatsko Family Archives. Painting of George and Mary Yatsko used to augment the poem, "Soft Pocket Hercules" by Emil Yatsko. Thanks also to Mike Swann and Mark Shackleford and Sam Samano, and to Joseph Hoover, SJ, at *America, the National Catholic Review.*

Photograph of Nicholas Campbell on back cover by Herb Gottesman © 1993; bio photo taken in 1984 at Cal State Northridge, © 1984 by CSUN. Blurb on the back cover by Ben Saltman from the original publication of this book, used by permission of Garden Street Press, © 1993. Special thanks to my brother, Michael Sheen Campbell, and to my mother, Ann Yatsko Campbell (b.1915-d.2010). Thanks also to poet Lawrence Spingarn at Los Angeles Valley College, and to late poets Ann Stanford and Benjamin Saltman at CSUN, and to Helen and Marjorie Saltman. Additional information noted at the end of this publication *Dandelion Clocks.* Copyright © 1993 and 2016. ISBN 13:9781497343634; ISBN 10:1497343631.

To my mother and father,

Ann and Harry G. Campbell,

and to my brother, Mike.

And to Ben Saltman, teacher and friend.

TABLE OF CONTENTS

DANDELION
CLOCKS POEMS
BY NICHOLAS CAMPBELL

You

Whatever road you happen
to be on you go that way.
All the world lies ahead.
Anyway you go you feel the way
one road connects with another.
Two towns become one.
Yet the way two people traveling
the same road arrive at different places.
The way grass points where the wind blows
yet remains part of the earth.

Shadows

Some things never happen
like the sun or the truth of some matter
coming to light.

We make them doing nothing more
than being ourselves.
Each time I move my shadow moves me.

One of my shadows is crossing
and re-crossing that road I take
that is a road my shadow takes
which someone is crossing and re-crossing.

We don't notice night coming on
but then we look around us.
It's hard to see at first what is there.

Shadows listen to the sun—
I learned this sitting under
a tree one day not moving.

Going Home

Here is the little stone
that broke away from a mountain
and that I rolled before me down
the road away from home so long ago.
This was a mountain once
that I pushed before me with my shoe.
Wherever home is I sit and watch
and wait for it to move.

Ceremony

In June there was a shot—
The screen door banged open
and the race began.

All summer we were in and out
until running was a ceremony
in which we ran back and forth
across the years,
the screen door waving goodbye.

Running, you think:
"We have all summer,
and even a day can seem long."

Some days summer lasts forever.
Mine banged open and closed.

The King

He wasn't supposed to move
but couldn't hold still
and I felt like that,
so when he sang I listened.

"Sit still," my parents said;
"Take your seat," the school insisted,
until I felt like a tree in a storm
struggling to free itself.

But the King understood,
though when he was drafted
and the Army cut his hair
Pat Boone fell out.

The world's changed now; it had to.
"Nothing stands still for long,"
I was told but wouldn't listen.
"Sit still," my parents said.

Hail And Farewell

San Francisco, California, February, 1988

Some boys on a street corner
were ready when I came along,
but not on this corner with these boys
crowded around a firecracker.

"Hello!" it said and I jumped
as boys ran in every direction.

One of them stopping said,
"We're sorry Mister," and I walked on
but looked back, once down another street,
years from where I stood waving goodbye.

River

A long mirror
in which I flow. Each year
my face grows more distorted,
my eyes less clear.

A child that comes here
grows old in me.
I begin as a spring and run
downhill to the sea.

My waves bend back,
I throw myself on the shore
to change what I am
to what I was before.

Horseshoes

You walk along a trail
and they appear
as if thrown from years.

Like so much of life: a game
in which our lives are pitched
at a stake in the ground.

They hang above doors
and we gallop under them
until our luck runs out.

The Boat

An empty boat that seemed
to be waiting the way a shore
at evening asks someone to walk there
nudged the pier nudging me.

Oars like arms thrown aside,
detached, suggested a sleeper
the sky had shaken, rousing the tide.

Far down shore a house, darkened,
alone, seemed to sigh but it was the waves,
as if I had opened the door of a room
and looked in on the sea
as it rolled over in its sleep.

Then a notion to untie the boat
seized me but it was the moment
I let go.

Soft Pocket Hercules

For thirty years my immigrant grandfather worked
for Andrew Carnegie whose task Carnegie said was
to make steel and bend it and my grandfather
already with the task of raising a family in a country
he'd never seen and that spoke a different language.

Immense, a life of bending steel and raising a family
for the world, giving still after all he had done what
he could of love, so immense he lifted himself in our
eyes above even the meanest task.

Meeting

I made this happen by coming here.
Today I arrive having yesterday come along
in that way only I could have come.

And you being who you are arrive
where you too must be,
there in that way being who you are today
only you could have come.

Then comes a day being in the world
each seeing his way the other's way
comes into view where say
only we could have come.

What My Sister Said

"Nobody cares," my sister said.
She was fourteen and meant
our parents didn't love her.
If I can't stay over Janie's I'll die," she said,
but meant they'd be sorry if it killed her.

"I hate this," she said,
but meant, "I'm going to cry."
"I'm going to cry," she said,
but meant, "I hate this."

"You know you're my friend
and I'd love a Coke," she said,
but meant if I was really nice
I'd go to the store for her with my nickel.

"My boyfriend's name is Nathaniel,"
she said, but meant she wrote his name
on the covers of her school books to hide
those old grocery bags.

"I'll get out of here someday," she said,
but meant, "I'll always be your sister.

Dream Time

My mother winding a clock said,
"This one we'll only wind but not set again."
It was always slow but ours,
and time didn't fly.

As I grew older there were other clocks
but this one said I was always a child.

Whatever I've done with my life
I set one clock for dreams.
Whatever time it says it's right.

Stone's Throw

"It's not far," you said.
As far as we could see
were railroad tracks and sky.
"I'll never leave," I said
and threw a stone over my shoulder
to seal it and went home.

"Say goodbye," you said,
but I said, "No," but we moved
anyway. We were only kids then,
it's all behind us, though now
I can see it was the stone
that threw me over its shoulder.

In Dreams

Every night you fall asleep
you lose your hold on the world.
Say you have a dream
you're a child again;
your sneakers stop you
from sliding off the roof.

But in the real world it rains.
Snow descends as you begin to slip
a little each day toward yourself.
You let yourself fall, knowing
whatever hold you have
on the world is a dream.

A Picture Of Heaven

Though everything it touches is transformed
not even snow can imagine heaven,
snow won't accommodate our idea of it.

Designers of windows,
we invite winter but stand ready with shovels
to clear the sidewalks and roads into April,
for we're reminded that nothing lasts,
and whatever snow touches becomes snow.

The Clocks

Time is money
but for all there is we're poor;
the little you steal
they won't pay you for.

Leaves are a clock
in a tower.
The grass: all our lives
somebody mows in an hour.

Fecund, the clock broods,
its eggs break at the touch of a hand.
The years are minutes, a life-sand.

A miser, he spent himself like a bee
and we felt his sting for all his honey,
his breath was an asset he wasted
making money.

Though her brain weighed a pound
and at the end she tried,
the whole weight of her genius
couldn't save a moment when she died.

We're clocks on a shelf.
Life is a spring a child winds
until he's old
and breaks himself.

The dandelions,
those delicate clocks,
have gone to seed.
I laugh as the wind blows.
How the years fly.

Pocket Change

My father as magician,
his illusion of crickets,
never failed to amuse us.
We never had any money,
but he knew the trick how
to make a few coins sing.

Who I Was

The future has entered through a hole in the self. Something lost, escaped from the blood in my lungs will not leave me alone but returns for me.

Changed, I grow sad but continue on my way, carrying this body, convinced it is no longer mine.

Whatever has happened someone who looks like me enters a room in the past, someone with my voice is talking or laughing somewhere, but it isn't me, though I must remember.

Even now my shoes feel strange. The future sets one foot inside me and I walk out of myself.

The Moth

A flicker in the woods
yet enduring as those trees.
This twice-spawned leaf
makes you believe you can
almost catch light in your hands.
Whatever root it takes depends
on what foot becomes a flower.

Brief bliss, whose moth life holds
close to the flame, this little worm
with wings, so that time may show
us what once crawled can fly.
Every time one passes
the sky waves goodbye.

A Mirror

When you look into a mirror
you say, that's me,
and the mirror goes on
being a mirror in the way
it has of being you.
You're all there is.

But turn away and a mirror
becomes something else:
a wall, a color,
but always a mirror
in the way a mirror has
of being a mirror.
It's all there is.

The Mirror's Other Side

You straighten a mirror,
the mirror straightens you.

You look twice.
You look but see how
you once looked.

A mirror sees what is
and what was.
Even a mirror has its mirror.

The Poem Is An Eye

The poem is an eye
through which the child sees
the world for the first time,
every time.

The paradox of more
being less: all these stars,
and yet this darkness.

The eye believes
but the hand doubts.
The hand sees
what the fingers
only with a touch imagine.

The mouth is an eye
that opens whenever
the tongue wants to see.

The eye needs light
to see, but the eye
could not see if it
were not itself light.

Summer School

In June we carved branches
into whistles, testing the sound
so that, when winter came,
we could bring down the cigar box
and breathe a little easier.
Summer taught us a song,
what we touched we remembered,
careful to carve a place for each finger.

The Chair

The carpenter's hands used him
until they made their occupation a man
who was nothing more than occupied.
But something he lacked
wouldn't let him rest;
some thing he couldn't still
was never enough, drove him on
until his life nearly done
he made a chair and sat down.

The Mosquito

In autumn the hammocks are left up, an offer of reparations but never surrender.

Arms and legs, the indiscriminate heat of August still lingering, we try to remain neutral and remove to the house, but there's a hole in the screen.

Our children, ambassadors, offer him their arms while the neighborhood dogs choose simply to close their eyes.

Claiming the plants, the mayor appears undisturbed as he sits on the porch applying the essential oils of his office, but even the ferns are eaten.

A petition is being circulated and signed with blood, but we know the country will never be at peace.

Glimpse

A spring before spring, Grandpa made flowers
from crepe and pipe cleaner and planted them
along the road for us to find.
Long winter had made us sad.

"When will it be spring?" we asked.
"Soon," he answered, but snow fell,
until one morning he said, "It's spring, children,"
and it was, like that August he brought milkweed
in the house: a winter before winter.

The Big Picture

"Long life," my uncle said, summer was almost over,
and he gave me some candy knowing I wanted it to
last forever.

Flavors varied as their colors, I held the package
noting my choices and a word stamped in my
memory and that I repeated as often as his name.

The matinee ended, we shared wafer after wafer,
knowing it wasn't the end of the world.

"Necco," I said, and we waited, loving every moment
it happened.

Leaving Wrightwood

A week in the mountains
and tomorrow already it's back
to the city and school—
Something will happen: a miracle.
We pray, hoping someone will listen.
Somebody does and it snows.

In the morning the cabin door
is forced open and the roads are lost.
We plunge our hands into the snow.
But then from the trunk of the car
the snow chains appear, symbols
of parental government, indifference,
and again we feel a sense of betrayal.

Parents, even when they're God
never understand this.

Where You Are

Anytime I'm alone everyone
in the world is somewhere others go
but where I don't want to be.

But when I'm lonely I'm never alone.
I can't be myself, the way I like being me,
knowing right where the others are.

All I want is to be myself.
You know that place where I go
but where you can never be.

I'm some place you can't imagine,
except when you're alone like me,
where love is any time you're happy.

A Short Walk

It's evening and the leaves have come far into the distance of other trees. After supper the chairs standing away from the table remind me of our own distances. Even my short walk outside to watch first stars I feel myself moving toward them as lights appear in windows; and though the pigeons under the eaves sound cold, I'm certain of having come nearer someone.

Transient

It's my belief
and true of the plum
that bears no fruit,
it's still a plum by its leaf.

If some flowers are not flowers
we need only a bee to show us
how to wrest honey from a weed.

Pigeons are those vagrants
in the park we love to feed.

Upward from birth
these are men whose roots
grow above ground whose branches
grow into the earth.

They've crossed the line
where we all pass from one
place to another, where
even the line must move on.

Address To An Onion

We understand though we express it with intimacy of human suffering this separable nature of yours, but it's for ourselves we mourn and foolish to think we truly understand such loss, such close concentric grief and sacrifice; and because it is ourselves we hurt, the whole world grieves for you.

Butterfly Collection

We just wanted to be friends, we said, startling the butterflies and never meant to harm them or each other, but wanted among our possessions some tangible light, some assurance we could show the world; but as we tried to capture a life, it somehow separated and we understood too late how impossible feelings are to preserve with the intention of pins.

Butterfly Scripture

"Inside the butterfly is a scripture."
Graffiti on a wall in San Francisco; ca.1967

Without words the butterfly is
itself. This is what air is, it says;
flicker of wings is all.

However I try to see anything
words come to mind, as now
this butterfly becomes a word.

Yet I see the sky writing a word
that is born out of nature's mind
as if some emblem of the soul.

Without words nature's mouth
opens and from it life flies,
transcending even life itself.

Without words the wordless
butterfly is gone,
leaving only our memory of it.

Rule Of Thumb

For Robe Barnhart

A boy down the street was right
when he said you can't shoot marbles
with a broken thumb.

Somewhere an outstretched hand
may still influence a driver to stop.
Nowadays it seems no one will stop for you,
even with a broken thumb.

When I held my hand up to say goodbye
I meant it, so it wouldn't hurt,
but this time I really mean it.

I once believed this was a world
where anyone would lend you his,
if you broke a thumb.

Please give it back, world,
that hand.

The Windows

Here were the family photographs we showed the world every day. Whenever we gathered in a room we made sure there was enough light and drew a shade when there wasn't, but sometimes we forgot and somebody took one—

"We want that photograph," we said and traded them now and then for the ones we took of our neighbors when they weren't ready. But they kept taking them and so we moved.

And as we carried out the furniture and they were sure we were leaving, they sorted our faces from the neighbors' or replacing them with others they were lost, and we took theirs out and left them behind.

Sueños de Nubes

An artist paints clouds
on a blue chair
and sets it in a room.
The chair is a dream
trying to be a room
with a chair in it,
and blue sky and clouds.
For a moment the room
begins to drift.
There is a feeling of light
making sense of things.
Then you notice a window,
and chair and sky merge.
Wherever you sit
you feel yourself floating.

Some Thoughts About The Sun

Sitting on a step in the sun I feel sunny. Every part of me is warm. Though it's winter, the sun is here and I have all morning if I want to be still.

The sun is a sound. A wave from the trees reaches me. Somewhere winter sounds like winter.

As much as I love this I don't look at the sun. Some have said of it, "nothing new under the sun," but in this old light early eyes of flowers have opened I have not seen before.

Sentimentalizing The Village

We loved the thought of her wrangling chickens in the yard, into the house at night, the chickens in the window in the morning, the thought of her sleeping with chickens. But a young man, and one from the village; the thought of them in the yard, in the house at night, in the window in the morning, the thought of them sleeping in the same bed.

We loved the thought of her wrangling chickens in the yard, into the house at night, the chickens in the window in the morning, the thought of her sleeping with chickens. But we wouldn't forgive her, even after he'd gone and we thought of her alone, wrangling chickens in the yard, into the house at night, the chickens in the window in the morning, the thought of her sleeping with chickens.

L'événement

For Jocelyne Morales,
Fréjus, France

Some dandelions grew near a stone
and I thought of their youth
and the stone's age and apparent wisdom
and said, I would be the stone.

Then a breeze reminded me
of the white heads of dandelions
and I considered the proportions
of their experience
and the stone's immovable nature
and my own proportions grew immense.

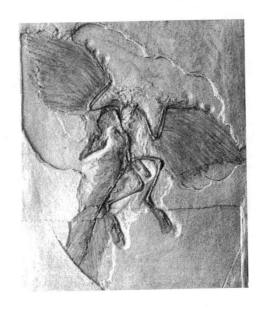

Solving The Old Conundrum
That Asks Which Came First,
The Egg Or The Bird?

If what some say is true
the egg was the first of the two.
A question not nearly as fantastic
as the lizard I've heard aspired so to fly
it became a bird.

Before bird was bird
or even wing was wing it was a leg
that, running from a leg,
dreamed it was a wing,
before the egg was egg.

Part

Here is a window so part
of the sky can be seen.

Whatever we mean, be it part
or whole, only part is ever seen.

Who among us has seen
the moon full and not seen half?

Only half the moon is seen,
only part is ever seen.

What is whole is always part.
Imagine eternity. Where do you start?

What mind has seen it?
Even eternity implies part.

Only part is ever seen.

Astronomer

Tonight I will open my telescope
while winter breaks the symmetry
of a pond. In the Koran it says the universe
is as close as the veins in our necks.

About Nothing

This isn't anything, it says.
But anything is possible.

This is the dream I have
about something in which nothing
could be anything.

Everything that is
will one day be this.

The poem goes on
being a poem without me.

Littoral

The young fisherman is dead
but only the sea understand this.
Like oars, his wife and children
miss his hands and fall silent.
Last night the nets in their throats
pulled hard, but the sea pulled harder.

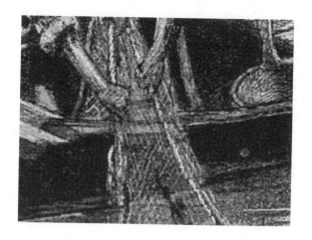

Sol In Homine

The sun is proof that truth
can be so common to be far from truth.

The sun is warm but not to all;
so large a thing can be so small.

Typical of sun is light
yet half the day is night.

Love

Every night a girl kneels
by the pools of the stars
pouring stars into them.

What is the rain but the stars
flowing into the sea.

All this dry land
and the stars around us
flowing constantly.

Poem From A Letter Written To Myself

Sometimes we don't know where we are but know where we're from but must go on to know where we were.

Something will happen you know will be better when pain's no longer an ambition.

Maybe your light has gone out but when it's dark enough it will shine.

I'll never love again, you say, but know there isn't anything in the flame that isn't in the moth, and love is all we have.

Learning To Fly

Sometimes you have to go far out on a limb for the fruit. You're afraid maybe, but then you love the world so much you're willing to fall. Once I reached that limb, high over a yard, up where I'd never gone. I wouldn't listen. When someone said, "come down," I said it was for love. "You'd better hold on," they said, but I didn't hear a thing, not even when she said, "I don't love you," I climbed out where love said, "Do it for me," until I was flying.

Dear World

Once in a cave someone wrote on a wall and though years passed before it was discovered, the past gestured, a hand moved across the years to greet us and a sound that may have been lost was heard.

Sometimes it happens: a friend will write or you'll read a poem and you're not alone anymore. Writing is a way the world has of not turning away. When we write we keep saying hello.

Barn Raising

Let utility be muse.
Inspire purpose. Use to any
desired end but let it be whole
in its parts as the simplest tool.
A roof forty-five degrees will carry
off the heaviest snow as a rule.
A roof that breathes, made
of wood that when wet
will allow one to see light
in a thousand places yet
not a drop of rain leak through.
Let it live, expand and contract.
Design is what a barn means.
Miscellany of animals, of house
and if scenes, doors ample with intent.
Beauty without embellishment.
Vivid as red paint; placed with sense
with a sense of place.
Let sunlight and wind devise
what direction it will face.
And when, some year, its color faint
this barn no longer in use,
let it be America's headstone.
Let north, south, and west face east *
like an old grave.
Let it like a spirit rise.

* Tombstones in traditional Western cemeteries usually face east. According to the Northumberland County Council, the tradition began when Pagans buried the dead so they would face the rising sun. Although modern cemeteries may have graves facing other directions, east-facing tombstones are still found in many traditional Christian and Jewish cemeteries. In America, especially before electricity came into use, barns were nearly always constructed door-side facing east to allow work to begin as early as possible.

The Demonstration

To the clash of cymbals and placards
they speak of small Tibet struggling
to gain its independence from China
and I think of how great China is
and these few people and shake my head.
Then I'm reminded of an ant struggling
to drag a moth across a sidewalk
and how impossible that appears.

Silence

I am nothing
therefore I am.

Now it grows even stiller,
somewhere beyond thought,
like the grass that hears
everything the sky hears
and even beyond its hearing.

Everyone who has ever lived
is around us, even now,
making this sound.

The Sky

Its endless way of being itself,
the sky says, "This is what today
is going to be and sometimes gray
is important, too."

But everything has its shadow,
even the sun.

Clouds are a dream the sky has
that it might prove
something so still can move.
If we can't see that far
at least clouds know where they're going.

In love with the grass and the sky's
blue nap, we wore a hole through
the world's old jeans.
But change, if forever,
is forever the same.

"How much of the sky do you want?"
it says; "You can have it all
and I'll still be the sky."

Poem

For Cammi Silk, Linnaea's Café, 1992

Everything has to end,
even this poem about love
that has no ending.

Without words spring
begins its own poem, like you
just beginning to be yourself.

Change is just something
that becomes something else.
Nothing has to end.

A Photograph Of Myself
At Age Ten, Taken By A Friend
At Jones Lake Near Shelbyville,
Indiana, Summer, 1959

Each second the world happens
and in that second the universe
moves: a water spider skates by
or the faint glimmer of a star.

Something you forgot appears,
a photograph of yourself staring
into a lake in whose shape you saw
even a wave can be still or the sky
hold its breath.

So a rock I skipped across the lake
goes on forever.

NEW POEMS

Child Of The World

When it snows his feet creak means
he wants to take a walk.

When it rings with his hand
he makes the telephone talk.

The sound of a hammer makes
nails go where it's dark.

A squirrel has a tail that's a question mark.

The yard waving means a butterfly is there.
Eggs are only where some chickens were.

The iron deer in the square
is always a fawn.

Some wheels make a road
as a man mows the lawn.

Shovel Ready
— For Sarah Samano

Love of the Great Pumpkin
is a shovel ready job.

A slogan chanted is not a slogan if it
is not a cry for the Great Pumpkin.

I'm not afraid of death now having helped
to bring into this world the Great Pumpkin.

Never a thought in the service of the Great Pumpkin
did I imagine digging my own grave.

Being buried under the Great Pumpkin would be
better than being buried under a swimming pool.

Thirteen is not unlucky if it is thirteen ways
of looking at the Great Pumpkin.

Actual Size

Growing up we were like grass
that nobody cut.
Our clothes fences we outgrew.
Every day without knowing
we wandered a little from ourselves,
but saw how even trees walked off
whenever leaves blew past.
Everywhere we went the town sighed.

The windows, once as big as lakes,
stood around our house in June.
There was a tree that was a tower,
a clock large as the moon.

But however big our town was
we knew its actual size: if you went away
long enough it changed.

Though the grass is tall
and in places comes to my knees,
the house where I lived as a child
has grown so small.

The greatest works of childhood
are often smaller than we know.
Perhaps all desire is a refusal
to see the world as it is.

Ah, but that new nickel

that your mother gave you,
and which you never spent
still says it's 1952.

Elegy For The Living

For Benjamin Saltman (d. 1999)

"He'll live on in his poems," someone said
of my old friend who is dying, as if he were
already a ghost haunting his books instead
of a house. I thought of a poem most like him
in which he had become a house and said,
"When he's gone I'll knock down every wall
and not find him. Can someone who has
lived, live on in a thing and be truly alive?"
And then I read his poem.

He was there. I heard his voice say he was a house
that "does not want to move," as I've
wanted myself to say: If I could be a house
someone could enter after I'm gone I'd be there.
If he'll sleep when this book isn't read
I'll read it every day to wake him.
As I've heard of a child I know who tries to wake her
dog by pouring water on its grave.

"Cleo's in the grass," she told her mother
and then said, "That's okay. That's okay,
grass is everywhere." And didn't I hear
my old friend say this but in another way?
"Now I'm here but then I'll be everywhere."
So he'll likely be: I'll carry his book everywhere
with me. Maybe I'll hear one morning as I read
a poem of his without dread of him being lost say,
"Holding on is as good as flying."

Image of poet Benjamin Saltman used by permission.
Special thanks to Helen and Marjorie Saltman.

Death is nothing at all. It does not count. I have only slipped away into the next room. Nothing has happened. Everything remains exactly as it was. I am I, and you are you, and the old life that we lived so fondly together is untouched, unchanged. Whatever we were to each other that we are still. Call me by the old familiar name. Speak of me in the easy way which you always used. Put no difference into your tone. Wear no forced air of solemnity or sorrow. Laugh as we always laughed at the little jokes that we enjoyed together. Play, smile, think of me, pray for me. Let my name be ever the household word that it always was. Let it be spoken without an effort, without the ghost of a shadow upon it. Life means all that it ever meant. It is the same as it ever was. There is absolute and unbroken continuity. What is this death but a negligible accident? Why should I be out of mind because I am out of sight? I am but waiting for you, for an interval, somewhere very near, just around the corner. All is well.

Henry Scott Holland, 27 January 1847- 17 March 1918, Regis Professor of Divinity at the University of Oxford

Lovers On A Porch In The Midwest

She pretends to listen to what he says though she'll remember every word when she needs to. One day he'll forget everything about this evening; he's already forgotten he's here in all his manners and verses.

She looks at him attentively as she plays with a flower that he brought her and that he picked from some neighbor's yard on his way to her house. She knows such spontaneity is the gesture of young men who believe themselves in love.

But on this summer evening, she'll let him believe his decision to come by and sit with her was his. What he's always wanted was to be here with her, to sit with no other and on no other porch but hers. Only them, alone, save for some locusts singing in the trees: "Pense menos mais," they sing.

Autumn Song
After Paul Verlaine

The wind can be so serious.
The trees lean toward evening.
Just when I think I know why
the wind blows the old year away,
it kicks leaves into the yard.

There is nothing sad in falling leaves,
only in saying goodbye to summer.
Nor is there any reason in saying why
leaves fall, except they must fall.

I burn leaves and watch them; the smoke
rises slowly and calms something in me.
I think of bees and take their example
as my own. Amid the smoke, there is a feeling
of great peace, yet I sense in it
the sun's savage simplicity.

Autumn is here only to explain the grasshopper's
burden and why it has an old face.
May I now state any grief I may note
in falling leaves is merely proportionate
to love or the lack of it.

1959

That year I made everything change
merely by looking away.

Done with a day I hid it, in here,
as a child might the entrance to a cave.

I would always be ten
and it was summer
in a small town where nothing
ever happened but trees.

Now no matter how far south they fly
even birds can't find it.

Some Trees

Those waves that break
somewhere on a shore are
only the wind making
what is near sound far.

Life being what it is,
a distant scene, I run toward
that far place. I always see myself
wanting only what is far.
Some birds arrive,
so I'll know the world over there
isn't a dream I have.

My attention lapses as it's snared
by a tree waving in the yard,
leaving an impression of a world
made entirely of sound, the sound
of the world asleep.

Dry leaves begin—
I hear the sound of rain
where there is no rain.

Sunflowers

What other name could such flowers
have and look so astonished?
That anyone might ask such a thing
and then run from a bee.

Never a thought of clouds
they move to face the sun.
Such attention to detail.
Together they look at me as one.

Like their namesake's long gaze,
what they must see!
To evoke in us such feeling might again
we stand among them as children?

As they grow toward the light
so we grow toward theirs.

Cake Or Death

Ten years old today, I'd like
all the cake in the world.
And while my sister promised me
her mustard sandwich, it's nice to know
most of us eat with our eyes.

A dime was all my father gave me
for my birthday. Tapping his way
through his cigarette, he said that ashes
are all we're left at the end.

And while new sneakers will lie to you
about the pace of youth, birthdays are good
if you remember it takes longer
to get to school if you walk backwards.

A cake that was a pair of dice
and that said I was ten meant I was lucky,
and birthdays are always better than death.

The gift I remember most was staying up
to watch the Army cut Elvis Presley's hair.
Then there was that mustard sandwich.

House Painter

He appears one morning adjusting a ladder
at a desired angle, as if adjusting the pictorial
grammar of the street. He looks at the clouds,
the weather of sheet upon sheet of canvas.
Who is he, someone asks from across the street,
or passersby. Children on their way to school
slow to watch him haul paint up a ladder
to the sky as if to perform some magic.

But if magician, he bares for all his sleight-of-hand.
Juggling paint and brush he conjures expertly
with deception of patience the most intricate
of tricks: a new house, where before was one
that was old. Perhaps his magic isn't magic
but the simple skill of washing clean the age
of something. If he can't prevent death
or control the rain, he heals without uttering
a word, though only a house is restored.

Concessione

In America the word bologna
is pronounced baloney, which means
don't believe everything you hear.
Bologna is film in cinema talk
while baloney is only a movie.

"*La Dotta* means the learned one;
La Grassa means the fat one,"
our Italian mechanic explains.

"*La Rossa*," he says, "refers to the red
roofs of our town." When we ask the cost
of the repair he says, "Don't ask
for axle grease if you want butter."

"Good work takes time and there is
always the cinema," he says.

While some of us love a movie,
others dine on film; but sometimes,
sometimes all you want is baloney.

Tribute

Don't ask who I am,
if you do I'll say,
I'm the awkward child
you knew yesterday.

Recollection be,
of time I was told,
and younger than he
would ever be old.

In youth far we see,
if in truth we can.
I never meant to be
a poet or a man.

End Remark

In our neighborhood we were known
as the ones the dragonfly made its own.
Try and touch us and you knew
how like it we in every direction flew.

Age has said, too, how like the hawk moth
childhood's wingspan grew,
though little notice it by us drew.

If reach exceeds youth's grasp
our grasp was true, so true youth is,
but half as new.

Biographical Note

Nicholas Campbell is of Slovak and Scottish descent. He was born in Greensburg, Indiana, in 1949, and attended Catholic and public schools in Indiana and California where he later studied verse writing at Los Angeles Valley College with Lawrence Spingarn and at California State University, Northridge, with poets Benjamin Saltman and Ann Stanford, and where, in 1984, he earned a Bachelor's Degree in English Literature. In 1988 he attended San Francisco State University where he worked on an M.A. in Creative

Writing studying poetry with Stan Rice. Campbell also attended California Polytechnic University in San Luis Obispo for two years. He has taught creative writing at the California Men's Colony, for Arts Reach at U.C.L.A., and for California Poetry in the Schools and participated in the summer writing workshops at Cuesta College near San Luis Obispo where he taught verse writing. The first edition of *Dandelion Clocks*, was published by Garden Street Press in 1993 and included many of the poems in this volume. Campbell now lives in Atascadero, California, where his brother, Michael, and he own and operate a European coffee house known as Socrates, next door to The Book Odyssey.

Mingo Junction, Ohio, ca. 1915, birthplace of Nicholas Campbell's mother, Ann Yatsko Campbell, March 23, 1915-April 30, 2010. She is buried at Mission Catholic Cemetery in San Luis Obispo, California.

Adams, Indiana, where Nicholas Campbell's father, Harry Guinn Campbell, was raised. He was born in Milroy, Indiana, one of three triplets, in 1910. He died in 1972, in Indianapolis, Indiana. He lies at rest in a small cemetery in Adams where his considerable family is also buried.

Harry Guinn Campbell, 1910-1972

Lúbime ťa a chýbaš nám, Mama

PHOENIX PRESS

For further information one may write to Nicholas Campbell at the address below:

Nicholas Campbell

5969 Entrada Avenue

Box 9

Atascadero, CA 93422

USA

58982753R00083

Made in the USA
Charleston, SC
23 July 2016